HISTORY AROUND US 1

Roman Britain

Warren Farnworth

Mills & Boon Limited
London, Sydney, Toronto

First published 1979

text © Warren Farnworth 1979

ISBN 0 263 06389 5

Filmset and printed in Great Britain by
BAS Printers Limited, Over Wallop, Hampshire
and bound by Hunter & Foulis Ltd, Edinburgh
for the Publishers Mills & Boon Ltd.,
17–19 Foley Street, London W1A 1DR.

Contents

Acknowledgements

The Publishers would like to thank the
following for permission to use photographs
from their collections (the numbers refer to
pages).

A. F. Kersting   31, 45, 63
Colchester Council   13, 48, 72 (right)
Warburg Institute   15, 34, 43, 67, 72 (left)
Society of Antiquaries of London   16
Crown Copyright Department of the
    Environment   12, 29, 30
Hunterian Museum, University of
    Glasgow   20
Barnabys   22
Corinium Museum, Cirencester   25
Butser Ancient Farm Project   26
Verulamium Museum, St. Albans   28, 36
Rowleys House Museum   32, 35
Museum of Antiquities, Newcastle upon
    Tyne   35
Janet and Colin Bord   37
National Monuments Record   35
Grosvenor Museum, Chester   39, 55
Reading Museum and Art Gallery Endpapers—
    27, 41, 51
National Museum of Wales   42, 44
Aerofilms Ltd   46, 54, 64
Colchester and Essex Museum   49
British Museum   21, 50, 55, 57, 71
City Museum of Gloucester   53
Picturepoint   59, 69
Edwin Smith Estate   61
Cambridge University Institute   68
Maidstone Museum   73
Yorkshire Museum   39, 74

Preface

This is the story of Roman Britain; a period of almost 400 years, beginning in the year A.D. 43, when much of Britain was ruled by the Romans.

All around us can be seen the remains of their occupation—roads, temples, walls and, in museums, their cooking pots, weapons and religious idols. All we have to do is know where to look and the past will speak to us.

Why they bothered to conquer this cold island in the north, no one really knows. Perhaps their Emperor, Claudius, wanted people to think of him as a great conqueror. Perhaps they thought of Britain as a land of fat cattle and rich mines which would bring them money. Or perhaps they wanted to punish the enemies of Rome who took shelter here.

Whatever the reason, we have much to thank them for. They gave our island a name—Britannia. They introduced us to glass windows, mosaic floors, central heating, postal services and sanitation. They showed us how to build towns and roads, how to dig canals, how to drain the fens and how to make watermills and aqueducts. They gave us an alphabet of letters which we still use today. Most important of all, by showing us how to govern, they helped to change a land of separate tribes into a nation.

Introduction

Hadrian's Wall near Housesteads
This is part of the great stone wall which the Emperor Hadrian ordered to be built when he visited Britain in A.D. 122. Here, looking eastwards towards the Roman fort at Housesteads, you can see what the wall looked like when it was finished.

The first Roman attack on Britain was led by Julius Ceasar. In the two swift invasions, the first in 55 B.C., the second the following year, he conquered the British tribes in the south east and marched on to the river Thames. Then he left, never to return.

The real conquest of Britain began much later, in A.D. 43, when four Roman legions, aided by auxiliary infantry and cavalry—a total of about 40,000 men, sailed from France. They were under the command of Aulus Plautius and after the main force landed safely at Richborough in Kent, the Romans began their attack.

At this time Britain was a land of many different tribes who often fought between themselves. Some of these tribes welcomed the Roman invasion, others surrendered without giving fight, but the remaining tribes, led by Caratacus and Togodumnus, stood and fought.

They were brave and fearless warriors, but no match for the powerful Roman army, and after a fierce battle at the river Medway near Rochester, they were routed. Togodumnus was killed, Caratacus fled to the west and the Romans marched on towards the river Thames to await the arrival of their Emperor, Claudius.

Claudius came and stayed for only 16 days in Britain, but it was long enough for

The vaults of the Roman temple at Colchester
Before the invasion of the Romans in A.D. 43, the most powerful chief in the south east of Britain was Cunobelin. He was so powerful that the Romans called him Britannorum Rex—the King of the British. His capital was Camulodunum (Colchester), so called because it was the fortress or 'dun' of Camulos, god of war.

The great stone temple which the Romans built at Colchester was destroyed during the revolt of the Britons in A.D 60. What was left of the second Roman temple which took its place was pulled down by the Normans when they built a castle on the same spot in the eleventh century, but these stone vaults on which the first temple was built can still be seen.

Roman Towns and their Modern Names

Aldborough
BRIGANTES

Brough on Humber
PARISI

Wroxeter
CORNOVII

Leicester
CORITANI

Caistor-by-Norwich
ICENI

Carmarthen
DEMETAE

Caerwent
SILURES

St. Albans
CATUVELLAUNI

Chelmsford
TRINOVANTES

Cirencester
DOBUNNI

Silchester
ATREBATES

Canterbury
CANTII

Winchester
BELGAE

Chichester
REGNENSES

Exeter
DUMNONII

Dorchester
DUROTRIGES

him to lead his army in triumph to Colchester—Camulodunum, as it was then called. Soon afterwards, the Romans built a great stone temple there, decorated with marble and alabaster, the first and largest Roman temple in Britain. It was built in honour of the Emperor Claudius, to serve as the centre for Emperor worship, the official religion of the Romans. Almost all of the temple is now destroyed, but the great stone vaults on which it was built can still be seen.

When the Roman army left their capital at Colchester and moved forward to conquer other parts of Britain, some of the older soldiers remained. They helped with the building and defence of the new town, which was to serve as an example of Roman civilization to the surrounding British tribes. One of them was a centurian called Marcus Favonius Facilis. His tombstone can still be seen in the museum at Colchester.

Here and there, as the Romans moved on, north towards Lincoln, west towards Gloucester and south towards Chichester and Exeter, they met fierce resistance. One great battle took place in A.D. 44 at Maiden Hill near Dorchester. The illustration on p. 54 shows how the hill fort looks today, and at the nearby museum at Dorchester you can see the skeleton of one of the fallen British warriors, his spine pierced with a Roman bolt.

But within six years, the Romans were in control of most of the British lowlands south of a line running from the river Trent to the river Severn.

Roman tombstone   Colchester and Essex Museum
This is the tombstone of Marcus Favonius Facilis, a centurian of the 20th Legion. When he died his two freed slaves—Verecundus and Novicius—erected this tombstone over his grave. It shows him in uniform. Over a tunic and kilt he wears a breast-plate, with a scarf tied around his neck to prevent chafing. His broad belt is studded with decorations won in battle and he carries a dagger and a sword. The vine staff he holds in his right hand is the symbol of his rank.

Skeleton of a British warrior   Dorchester County Museum

A great battle took place at Maiden Hill near Dorchester in A.D. 44. (You can see a picture of the hill fort, as it is called, on page 54). After opening fire with their artillery, showering the fort with heavy stones, burning missiles and iron bolts, the Romans launched their attack at the east gate. The legionaries defended themselves from the British archers and stone-slingers by closing ranks and raising their shields above their heads. In the clash of battle many men fell and the British were defeated.

The skeleton of this man, whose body was found in a shallow grave, shows that he was killed by a Roman ballista bolt which entered his body from the front and pierced his spine.

Wales, which they attacked next, was more difficult to conquer. Even after the capture of one of their leaders, Caratacus— the same Caratacus who escaped from the Romans at Rochester—the Welsh tribes would not accept defeat, and it was almost ten years before they were driven back to the island of Anglesey. With his legionaries and the Batavian auxiliaries (who were trained to swim in full armour, Suetonius Paullinus, the new Governor of Britain, crossed the Menai Straits and captured the island in A.D. 60.

Little can now be seen to remind us of this early campaign in Wales but at Y Pigwn, a desolate spot high on the mountains of south Wales, are the remains of a temporary camp built by the Romans.

The Roman victory at Anglesey was shortlived, for in the same year, news reached the Governor of an uprising in the south of England. Angered by their ill-treatment by the Romans, the Iceni tribe of East Anglia, led by their Queen, Boudicca, were in revolt. Colchester was under attack, and each day Boudicca's army grew larger, as neighbouring tribes came to her aid.

The statue of Boudicca   The Embankment, London

King Prasutagus of the Iceni tribe was one of the British chieftains who made peace with the Romans, and was allowed to rule his own lands in East Anglia. When he died in A.D. 59 he left half his kingdom to the Emperor Nero and half to his wife, Boudicca. Unfortunately, the chief tax collector in Britain demanded all of it and sent his officers to take it by force. Queen Boudicca was flogged and her daughters were assaulted, but the following year the Queen took her revenge.

No one knows what she really looked like and this statue of her in London only shows her as we might like to think of her, but a Roman writer called Dio Cassius said of her that,

'she was huge of frame, terrifying of aspect, and with a harsh voice. A great mass of bright red hair fell to her knees. She wore a great twisted golden necklace, and a tunic of many colours, over which was a thick mantle fastened with a brooch'.

Important towns in Roman Britain

Suetonius Paullinus acted quickly. Leaving his infantry to march south as fast as they could, he rode ahead with his cavalry. He reached London with time to spare—but with too few men. The reinforcements he expected from Lincoln and Gloucester failed to arrive. There was nothing he could do but retreat. Soon after, he was to defeat Queen Boudicca in a great battle fought somewhere in the Midlands (between Towcester and Atherstone on Watling Street), but not before her warriors had burnt Colchester, London and St Albans to the ground, and left thousands slain. Queen Boudicca escaped, but she later killed herself.

Suetonius Paullinus punished the Britons harshly and laid waste to great parts of Britain, but he was soon replaced by more sympathetic governors who set about rebuilding the burnt towns and brought life back to normal.

In A.D. 78, Julius Agricola, one of the greatest of all Roman governors, came to Britain. After finally subduing the Welsh, he led his army slowly northwards. By A.D. 80 they were in Scotland—Caledonia as it was then called—and four years later, under the command of Agricola, they defeated a Caledonian army at Mons Graupius in the far north of Scotland. (You can read about the battle which took place on page 60).

The Romans then retreated. They moved south to build new towns and frontier forts, and to rebuild the wooden defences of their important legionary fortresses at York, Chester and Caerleon, in stone.

After more than 50 years of Roman occupation, many of the tribes in the Midlands and the south of Britain had grown to accept their new way of life, and Britons began to live and work in Roman towns. (You can see a map of Roman towns on the opposite page.)

In Scotland and the north the tribes were more troublesome and from time to time, when the Roman army was off guard, they banded together and attacked. This was one of the reasons why the Emperor Hadrian, who visited Britain in A.D. 122, ordered that a great barrier be built from the Solway to the Tyne. We call it Hadrian's Wall.

HADRIAN'S WALL   Sites to Visit

1 Carlisle: Museum
2 Birdoswald: Wall fort
3 Willowford: Wall and turret
4 Poltross Burn: Milecastle
5 Walltown: Wall
6 Greatchesters: Wall fort
7 Cawfields: Milecastle
8 Housesteads: Wall fort, with granaries, hospital & latrine
9 Chesterholm: Fort
10 Carrawburgh: Wall fort, with good view of the vallum
11 Chesters: Wall fort
12 Corbridge: Roman town and supply depot
13 Halton: Fort
14 Rudchester: Fort
15 Benwell: Temple
16 Newcastle upon Tyne: Museum
17 South Shields: Fort and museum

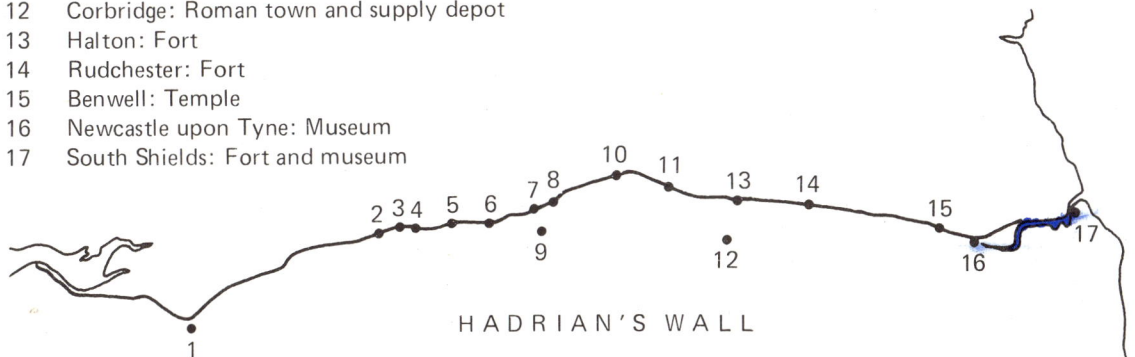

HADRIAN'S WALL

Antonine Wall plaque   Hunterian Museum, Glasgow

After the building of Hadrian's Wall and the death of Hadrian in A.D. 138, the new Emperor, Antoninus Pius, ordered the building of another wall across the narrow neck of land between the Forth and the Clyde. It was called the Antonine Wall after the new Emperor. Nearly 60 kilometres long, it was built of turf on a stone foundation and was fronted with a deep ditch.

Like Hadrian's Wall, it was built by the Roman soldiers, and this distance slab tells us that part of the wall was built by men of the 20th Legion. In the centre of the slab you can see a Roman standard bearer bowing to Britain (in the shape of a lady), with a defeated Briton on each side, and the Legion's symbol of a running boar beneath.

It stretched for 115 kilometres and for much of its length it was three metres thick and up to four metres high, not counting the parapet. In front of the wall, to the north, lay a great ditch, nine metres wide and nearly three metres deep, except where the steep cliffs made it unnecessary. Behind the wall, to the south, there was another ditch called the vallum, which helped to control frontier traffic. At intervals of one Roman mile (about one and a half kilometres) small forts were built and between each fort were two square turrets

used as watchtowers. The forts, or milecastles as they are called, were large enough to house about 30 auxiliary soldiers who were responsible for patrolling their section of the wall. In addition to this, 16 larger forts, each capable of holding 500 or 1,000 troops, were built on or near the wall on the south side, and some of these forts were connected by a road known as the Stanegate.

Seventeen years later, the Romans moved further north, and built another barrier, the Antonine Wall, which stretched from the Forth to the Clyde.
(Maps on pages 19 and 21 show some of the many interesting sites which can still be seen today, on or near the two great Roman walls.)

But walls were not enough to keep the tribes in check. In A.D. 180, the Antonine Wall was abandoned. It was too weak, too far north and there were too few soldiers to defend it.

Time and again, the Romans found themselves faced with warring tribes from both sides of Hadrian's Wall, who attacked as far south as York itself. Peace in the north was not finally restored until the

Emperor Severus arrived in Britain in A.D. 208, and his son, Caracalla, defeated the Caledonian tribes. Once again, Hadrian's Wall became the northern frontier and Britain was at peace for almost a century.

Roman coin   British Museum, London
The Romans were never a great seafaring nation. When they conquered, they conquered with the might of their army, but a small navy was always necessary to patrol rivers, protect the coast, and to transport men and supplies across the seas.

In Britain, docks and harbours were built around the south and east coast. A fleet of warships—like the one shown on this coin—was kept busy guarding the trading ships which passed to and fro between the ports of York, London and the continent.

This map shows where the remains of the Antonine Wall can best be seen

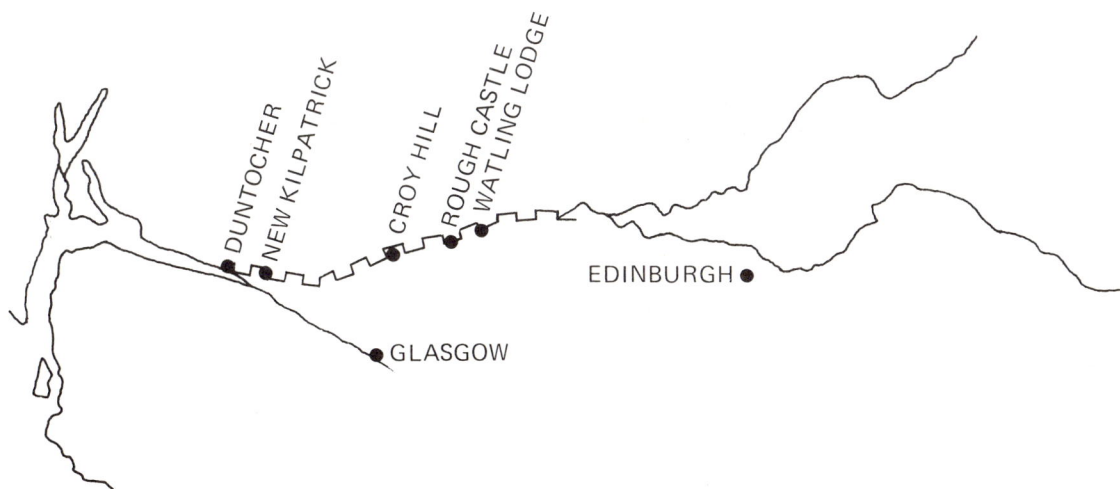

The next threat came not from the land, but from the sea, when Saxon pirates began to raid and plunder on the east coast of Britain. To meet this new danger, the Roman Fleet was strengthened, and coastal forts were built from the Wash to the Isle of Wight. Tiles found at Dover, stamped with the letters CL BR (short for Classis Britannica, meaning British Fleet) tell us that Dover was then the Fleet headquarters. The lighthouse there can still be seen. Of the many coastal forts which were built, remains can be seen at Richborough, Portchester, Pevensey and Burgh Castle. (See map on page 24)

As the Saxon raids continued, more coastal forts were built in the east, and a commander of all naval operations was appointed, with the title—Count of the Saxon Shore. By the middle of the fourth century, Britain also came under attack from tribes in the north and the west, and in A.D. 367, the enemy made a combined assault.

In the north, Hadrian's Wall and its forts were overthrown by the Picts from Scotland, Scots from Ireland attacked Wales, and Saxons landed in the south and the east.

Count Theodosius was sent to Britain by the Emperor to restore peace. He drove back the invaders, rebuilt Hadrian's Wall and erected signal towers along the Yorkshire coast to watch out for Saxon raiders. The remains of one of the inland towers can be seen on Bowes Moor in County Durham.

In A.D. 383, Magnus Maximus, the Duke of Britain, and commander in chief of the northern frontier, rebelled against Rome and took many soldiers away from Britain to help him in his fight to become the new Emperor. Although he was later captured and put to death, his army never returned and much of Britain was left undefended.

By the year A.D. 400, Hadrian's Wall was again overrun. The signal towers on the Yorkshire coast were stormed by Saxon raiders and the few Roman troops remaining in Britain were called back to defend Italy from the Goths. Rome itself was threatened. In A.D. 410, when the British leaders asked the Emperor for help, he told them to defend themselves.

After living under Roman rule for so long, the Britons had few natural leaders, but one such was called Vortigern. He rallied the people together, held the Scots and the Picts at bay and allowed groups of Saxons to settle on the east coast, in return for their help in driving off other Saxon invaders. In time, more and more Saxons came, demanding more and more land, until they were strong enough to turn on the British and take the land by force.

About A.D. 450, the Britons made one last appeal to the Romans:

> To Aetius, thrice consul, come the groans of the Britons . . . the barbarians drive us into the sea, the sea drives us back to the barbarians; between these two means of death we are either killed or drowned.

They received no answer. It was the end of Roman Britain and the beginning of another story in our history—the story of the Anglo-Saxons.

The Roman lighthouse at Dover
This is the lighthouse which the Romans built at Dover, once the headquarters of the Roman Fleet. It stood 27 metres high, but now only 20 metres remain. (The neater looking stonework at the top was added in medieval times.) Ships using the English Channel by day were guided by a column of smoke from the top of the lighthouse, at night a beacon fire was lit.

24

SAXON SHORE FORTS

1 BRANCASTER
2 BURGH CASTLE
3 WALTON CASTLE
4 BRADWELL
5 RECULVER
6 RICHBOROUGH
7 DOVER
8 LYMPNE
9 PEVENSEY
10 PORTCHESTER
11 BITTERNE
12 CARISBROOKE

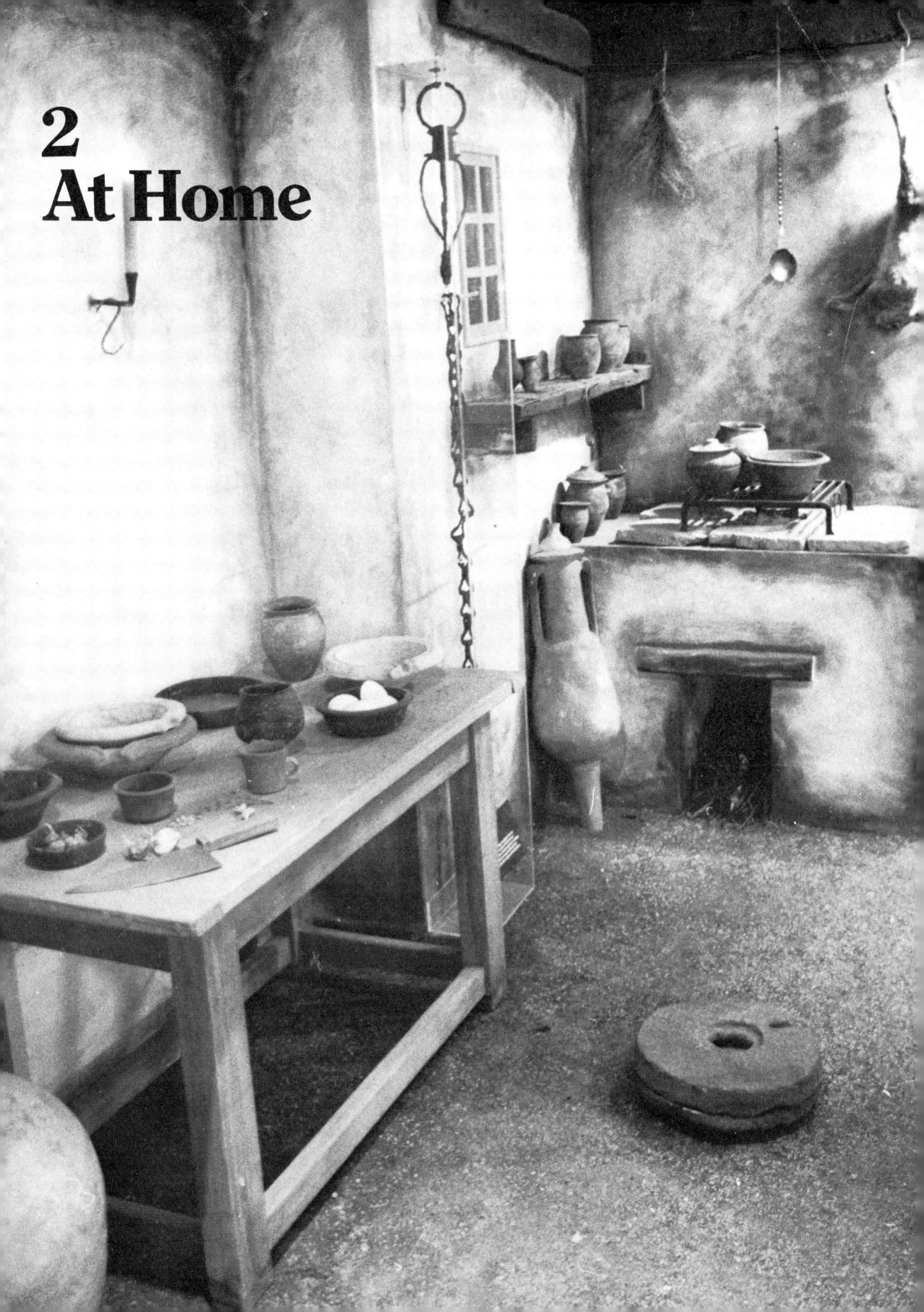

2
At Home

(Previous page)
Roman kitchen   Corinium Museum, Cirencester
This is the kind of kitchen in which a Roman woman
would cook her husband's supper. If he was fairly
wealthy, he would expect to come home to a three
course meal beginning with eggs or shellfish, followed
by roast beef or mutton served with a spicy sauce,
salty with anchovies and yellow with saffron. To finish
off, there might be a sticky, honey-flavoured pudding
or dried figs imported from abroad. To eat all this, he
would use his fingers and a spoon. Forks were
unknown and knives were seldom needed because the
meat was usually cut up into small pieces.

A British family might only have a gruel made from
ground corn or a bean pudding seasoned with salt and
herbs, but they much preferred to have roast pork or
beef.

The Britons were farming people. At the
time of the Roman invasion, most of them
lived in small settlements containing a
cluster of houses, with outbuildings for
their cattle or sheep. The remains of some
of these simple homes can be seen at Ewe
Close in Cumbria, Tre'r Ceiri in Gwynedd
and at Chysauster and Halligye in

**Ancient British house   Butser Farm, near
Portsmouth**
This is the kind of house which many Britons lived in
when the Romans came to Britain. Inside it was dark
and smoky. There were no windows and hardly any
furniture. A corner of the house was screened off to
make a sort of bedroom, where everyone slept together
on animal skins on the floor. Weapons were kept ready
for use in a cupboard just inside the doorway.

A Roman living room   Reading Museum
This is what a Roman living room looked like. The man who owned it was obviously wealthy because he could afford a patterned mosaic floor, painted walls and glass windows. Like most Roman rooms there was not much furniture. The owner sits on an upholstered leather couch made of wood and Kimmeridge shale (a slaty, coal-like material which could be turned on a lathe and polished). His wife has a wicker chair, whilst the children play on a fur rug. When it grew dark the room was lit with candles and small bronze oil lamps.

Cornwall. At Butser Farm near Portsmouth you can see a reconstruction of the kind of house which was used by people living in the Midlands and the south of Britain. It has a low, round wall of clay-covered wood or stone, and a cone-shaped roof covered with thatch or turf. A large house such as this, 14 metres high in the centre, would have belonged to a chief. Poorer people had much smaller houses.

Sometimes, a whole tribe of people lived on a hilltop protected with ditches and pallisades. Examples of these can be seen at Danebury in Hampshire, Maiden Hill in Dorset and The White Caterthun in Angus.

A tribal capital such as Camulodunum had streets with hundreds of houses, workshops and temples, but it was nothing compared to the towns which the Romans built. Thatched houses and settlements might be good enough for the Britons, but Romans preferred the civilized life of the town and the comfort of a 'real' house, for

even a small Roman town house was much better than a native hut. The walls were built with a wooden frame, filled in with wattle and daub, and the roof was tiled.

Inside there was a living room and a dining room, one or more bedrooms, a kitchen and a storeroom. The dining room (the most important room in the house) might have a concrete floor and a painted ceiling, like the one you can see in the museum at St. Albans.

Painted ceiling   Verulamium Museum, St. Albans
Many Roman houses and villas were richly decorated
with paintings and mosaics. This painting of doves and
panther heads once covered the ceiling of a house in
St. Albans.

Latrine at Housesteads fort on Hadrian's Wall
This soldiers' latrine can be seen at Housesteads, a
Roman fort on Hadrian's Wall. There was no privacy.
Soldiers sat side by side on wooden seats over the deep
sewers running down each side of the building. Toilet
paper had not been invented. Soldiers cleaned
themselves with a sponge on the end of a stick which
they dipped into the narrow channels of water at their
feet. Then they would wash their hands in one of the
two stone washbasins in the centre of the room.

Towns also had public lavatories like this one.
Usually they were in the bathhouse where a constant
flow of water was used to flush the lavatories into the
town sewers. If there was no public lavatory, people
made do with an earth closet at the back of the house,
or took advantage of large jars which fullers placed at
street corners. Fullers collected the stale urine and
used it to remove grease from newly-made woollen
cloth.

Even Roman soldiers lived in much better
conditions than the native Britons. At
Housesteads, a fort on Hadrian's Wall, you
can see their stone-built latrine; and at
Chesters, another fort nearby, there is a
bath house complete with lockers for the
soldiers' clothes.

A wealthy Roman official, or a retired
centurian who had been given land outside
the town, built himself a country house or
villa where he could settle down with his
family and employ local Britons to work the
land. Some villas were very grand, others
were only small, but in time the richer
British farmers began to copy them and live

as the Romans did. The remains of many villas can still be seen today, but one of the best to visit is at Chedworth in Gloucestershire. There you can see the dining room with its fine mosaic floor, a suite of five bathrooms, the hottest of which is heated by a hypocaust, a spring which supplied the villa with water; together with the remains of latrines and sewers. (The most important Roman villas and British houses and settlements are shown on the map on page 33)

Life for most ordinary people in Roman Britain began early—at daybreak. After a quick breakfast of bread and honey (the

(Right) **The hypocaust at the villa in Chedworth, Gloucestershire**
Some of the better Roman houses and villas had a hot-air central heating system called a hypocaust, making life more comfortable in Britain's cold, damp climate. Hot air from an outside furnace, fuelled with charcoal, flowed under the floors of the house (which were supported on stone or brick pillars) and up flues inside the walls. Here you can see some of the supporting pillars of the mosaic floor and some of the wall flues at the bottom of the far wall.

(Below) **Soldiers' bath-house at Chesters fort on Hadrian's Wall**
This fort was once the home of auxiliary cavalrymen from Spain. This is their bath-house where they came to wash themselves and relax. The five niches in the wall on the right were lockers for their clothes.

British preferred porridge) washed down with home-made beer or watered wine, they were off to work. Farmers to their fields, townspeople to open their shops or offices and children off to school.

Of course, not all children went to school. British children hardly ever did, unless they were the sons of a chief or a rich farmer, but most Roman children who lived in large towns were sent to the local school—often just a small room behind a shop. (Only a wealthy Roman could afford to employ a private tutor to teach his children at home.) Boys started school at the age of six or seven, where they were taught to read and write Latin and do simple arithmetic on an abacus. Some would continue after the age of 11 or 12, to learn history and geography, Greek and geometry, and rhetoric (the art of public speaking). The teachers were very strict. Boys who were late for school, or failed to learn their lessons, were whipped or caned.

Women and girls stayed at home. There was much to do. Cleaning the house, filling the oil lamps, shopping for food (although much of the shopping was done by the husband), looking after the baby and preparing food.

At the Corinium Museum at Cirencester, you can see a reconstruction of a typical Roman kitchen. Much of the cooking was done over a charcoal fire on top of a stone hearth, but an open fire was used for roasting joints of meat on a spit, or making stews and soups in a cauldron. In the kitchen you can see some mortaria (dishes with a roughened inside surface) which were used for grinding herbs and spices, a quern stone used for grinding corn into flour and a double-handled container with a pointed base—called an amphora—in which olive oil was kept.

Roman inscription   Rowley's House Museum, Shrewsbury

The Romans not only taught the British how to read and write, they also gave them an alphabet of letters which we still use today. Compare the letters on this inscription with the capital letters used on this page. This stone inscription was placed over the entrance to a forum or market place which was built at Wroxeter in Shropshire in A.D. 130 and dedicated to the Emperor Hadrian.

The Romans also taught us how to count using these same letters, like this—

1	2	3	4	5
I	II	III	IV	V

6	7	8	9	10
VI	VII	VIII	IX	X

50	100	500	1000
L	C	D	M

If you had to write 1980 in Roman numerals, it would look like this—MCMLXXX.

This map shows where you can see the remains of villas, shops, markets, Roman town houses, latrines, hypocausts, wall paintings and mosaics, and pre-Roman settlements.

1	The White Caterthun, Angus	Pre-Roman hill fort
2	Housesteads, Hadrian's Wall	Roman latrine
3	Ewe Close, Cumbria	Pre-Roman settlement
4	Binchester, Co. Durham	Hypocaust
5	Tre'r Ceiri, Gwynedd	Pre-Roman settlement
6	Wroxeter, Salop	Market hall/latrine
7	Wall, Staffordshire	Hypocaust
8	Carn Euny, Cornwall	Pre-Roman settlement
9	Chycauster, Cornwall	Pre-Roman settlement
10	Halligye, Cornwall	Pre-Roman settlement
11	Caerwent, Gwent	Roman house
12	Somerdale, Avon	Roman villa
13	Great Whitcombe, Gloucs.	Roman villa
14	Chedworth, Gloucs.	Roman villa/hypocaust/mosaics
15	North Leigh, Oxfordshire	Roman villa/mosaic
16	St. Albans, Hertfordshire	Roman house/shops/mosaic/painting
17	Lullingstone, Kent	Roman villa/mosaic
18	Canterbury, Kent	Roman house
19	Dover, Kent	Roman house/painted wall
20	Bignor, Sussex	Roman villa/mosaic
21	Fishbourne, Sussex	Palace/mosaic
22	Horndean, Hampshire	Reconstructed British house
23	Newport, Isle of Wight	Roman villa
24	Brading, Isle of Wight	Roman villa/mosaic
25	Silchester, Hampshire	Roman house
26	Danebury, Hampshire	Pre-Roman hill fort
27	Rockbourne, Hampshire	Roman villa
28	Maiden Castle, Dorset	Pre-Roman hill fort

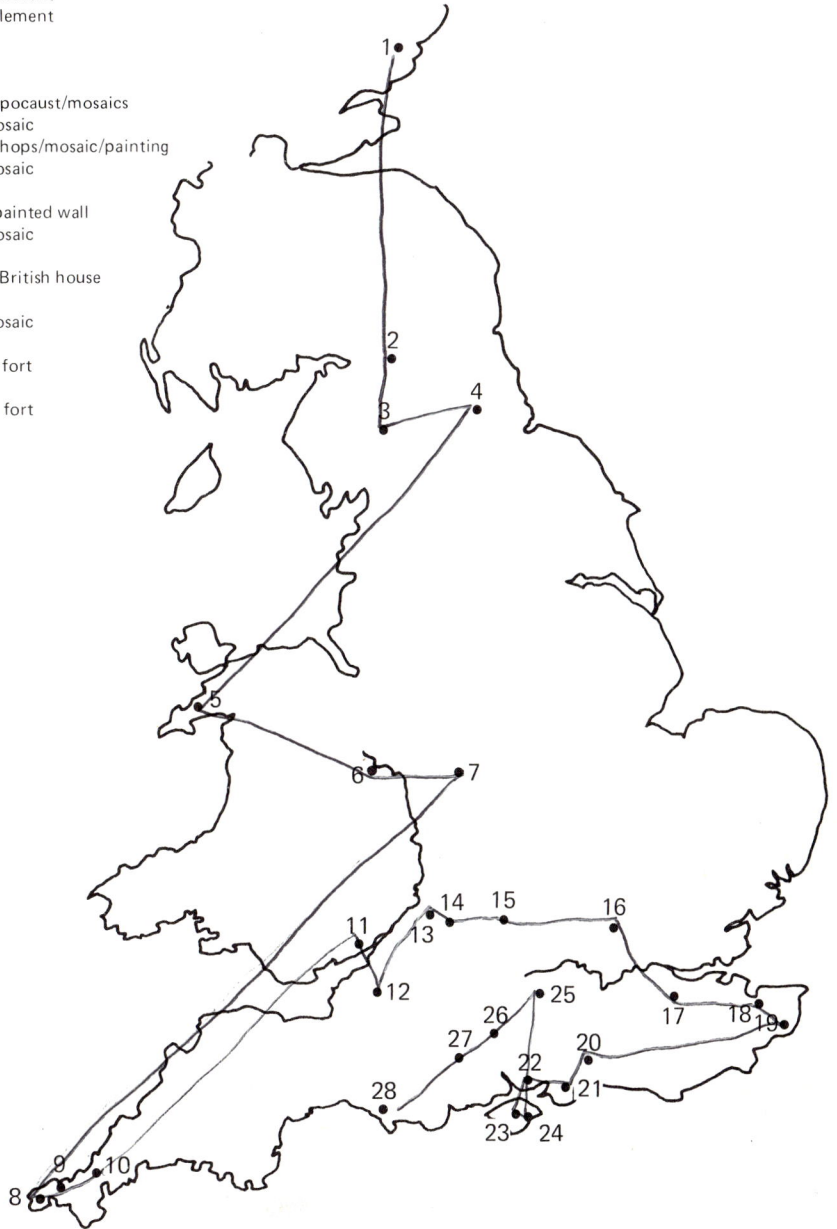

After lunch—usually a light meal of bread and cheese—most people went back to work, but those who had servants and slaves spent the afternoon strolling around the town, and perhaps meeting their friends at the public baths.

How did the people dress? The native Britons wore tunics of linen or wool, often dyed in bright colours and decorated with embroidery. Men usually wore trousers or leggings. On cold days, a cloak of striped wool or goat's hair was worn, fastened at the shoulder with a metal brooch.

The Romans were less fond of bright colours, but they too wore tunics of all kinds. Out of doors, women wore a long tunic with sleeves, called a stola and maybe a square cloak with a hood. Men also wore cloaks, but the formal outdoor dress for a Roman citizen was the toga—a length of fine, white wool which was draped over the shoulder, folded around the body and allowed to hang down the back.

Shoes, boots and sandals of all kinds were worn, but Roman women liked to wear elegant slippers like those which you can see in the museum at Vindolanda in Northumberland. Roman women also liked to dress themselves up, especially for an important dinner party. A rich woman spent a lot of time over this. Servants helped her to wash in scented water and rub her body with perfumed oils. One servant plucked her eyebrows and applied some eyeshadow made from powdered antimony and ash, whilst another manicured her nails. The lady herself applied the finishing touches of make-up, using chalk and white lead to whiten her face and neck, red ochre to colour her lips and tint her cheeks, finishing off with a spot of expensive perfume which her father had sent to her from Rome.

Tombstone   Yorkshire Museum, York
This Roman family, dressed in the sleeved tunics and thick woollen cloaks which people wore in a cold British winter, once lived in York. It was the family of Gaius Aeresius Augustinus, a veteran soldier who served with the 6th Legion. This tombstone was erected by him in memory of his wife, Flavia, who died when she was 39, and his two children who both died before they were two years old. The sculptor has carved the two children to look much older than they really were.

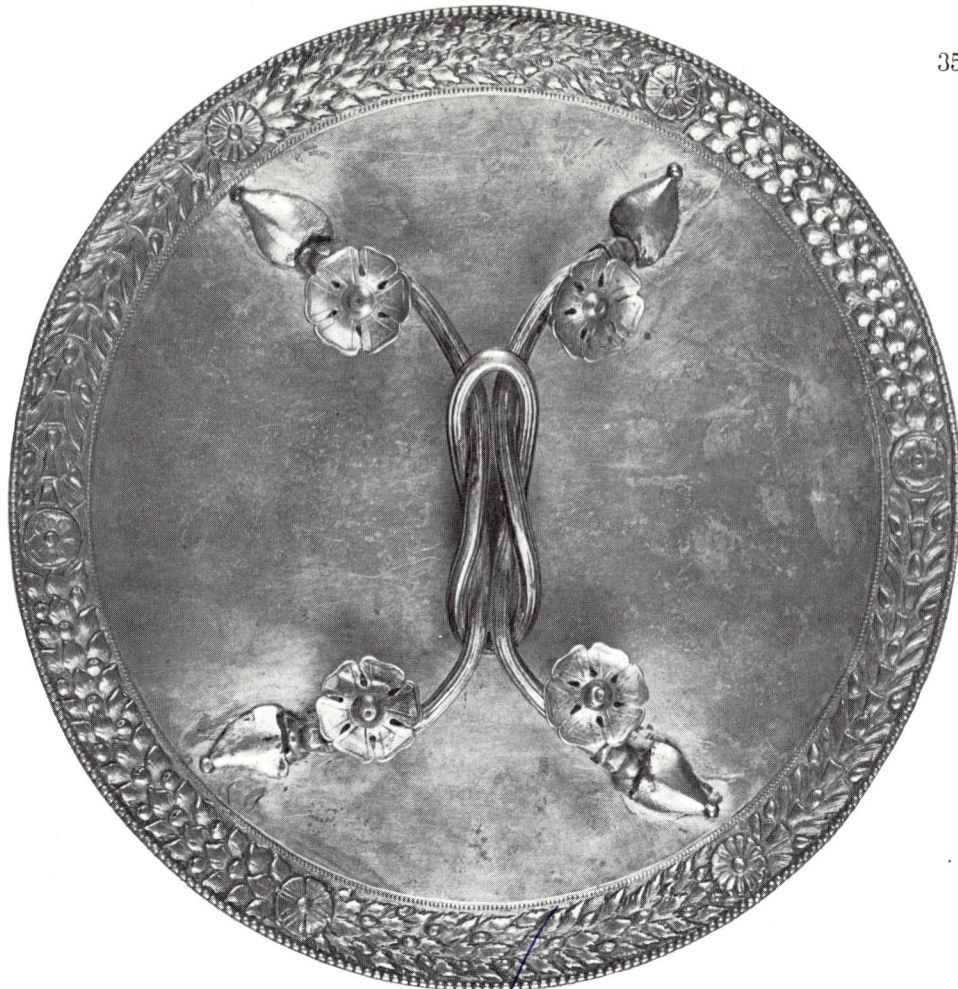

The Wroxeter mirror   Rowleys House Museum, Shrewsbury

A wealthy Roman woman looked into this mirror to admire her new hairstyle. Sometimes her hair was plaited and pinned up around her head with long pins of jet or silver; sometimes it was curled in ridges and decorated with strings of pearls.

British women wore their hair long. (Queen Boudicca's hair, we are told, hung down to her knees.) Sometimes it was left to hang straight; sometimes it was plaited, or drawn together at the back of the head—like a pony's tail.

Aesica brooch   Museum of Antiquities, Newcastle upon Tyne

This beautiful gilded bronze brooch, found at Greatchesters on Hadrian's Wall, may once have been the proud possession of a noble Briton. All Britons, men and women, loved to wear ornaments and jewellery. Women wore glass beads, rings of silver and jet, bronze pins and brooches, armlets, necklaces, enamelled pendants and decorated belts. Roman women too, wore fine jewellery—silver earrings, ivory bracelets and amber beads.

Statue of Venus   Verulamium Museum, St. Albans

For young Romans getting married was an important event, although it was often the parents who chose the marriage partner.

When a couple became engaged, the marriage contract was signed, the girl's father paid a dowry— usually gold or silver—to the young man's parents and gifts were exchanged. The girl might give her husband-to-be a ring engraved with the word A M I C A, meaning sweetheart, and in return the young man might give her a small statue of Venus, the goddess of love, like the one shown here.

The day before the wedding the young bride would offer her toys to the family gods who had taken care of her, and the house was decorated with flowers. (Under Roman law a girl could be married at the age of 12.)

The wedding itself often took place in the late afternoon. The bride was dressed in a long white tunic tied with a woollen girdle. Her veil and shoes were saffron yellow. After the marriage ceremony and the wedding feast the bride and groom, escorted by their relatives and friends, walked to their new home where the husband carried his bride over the threshold and the wife offered three coins; one to her husband, one to the household gods of their new home and one to the god of the nearest crossroads.

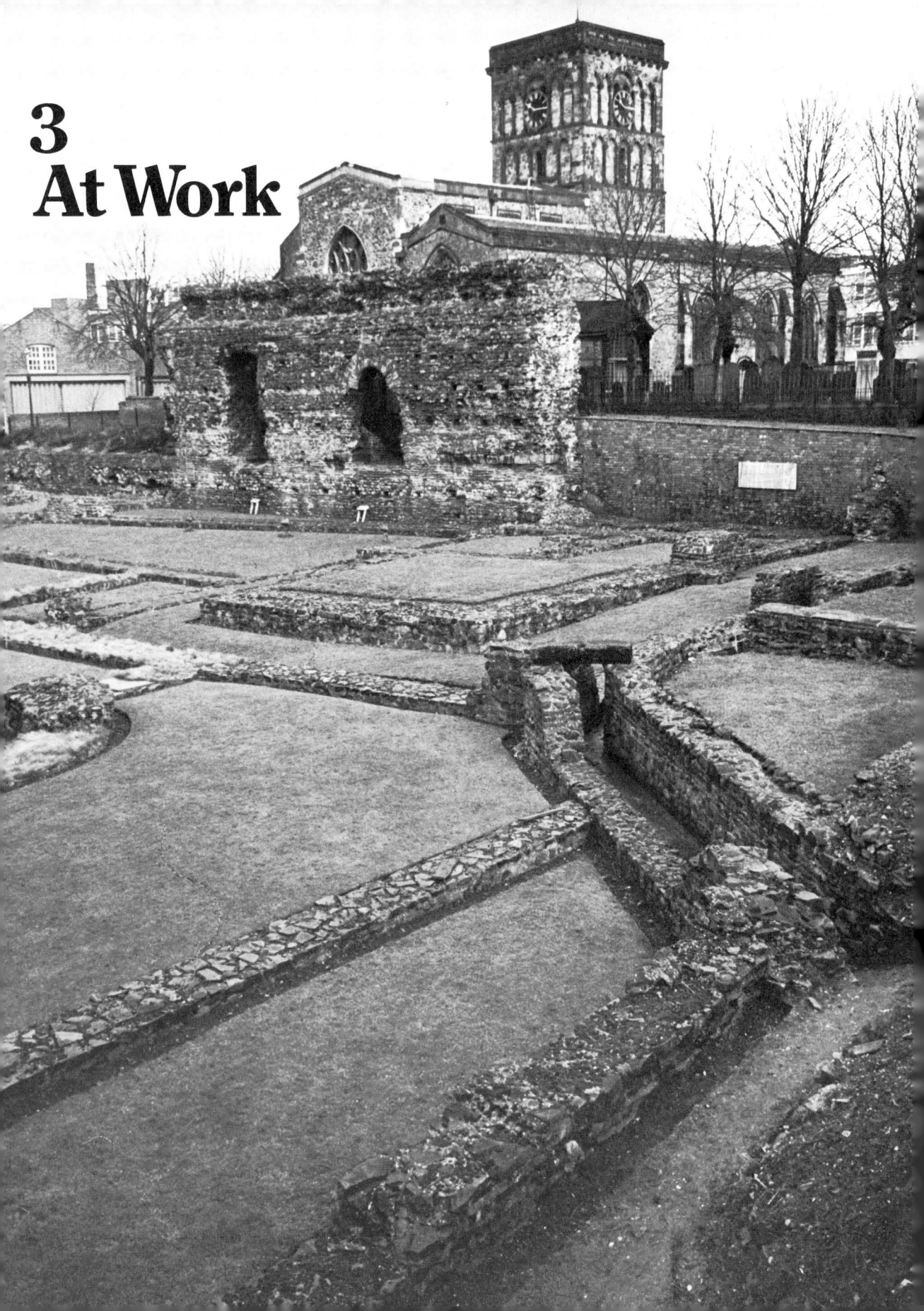

3
At Work

(*Previous page*) **The Jewry Wall, Leicester**
As the Romans advanced across Britain, they built temporary camps. These camps soon attracted the local Britons. Farmers and small traders found a ready market selling fresh food and vegetables, cheese and wine to the soldiers. Tribespeople found work as servants and labourers. In time, a small settlement of native huts, shops and stalls grew up around the camp and when the soldiers left, the settlement remained and grew into a small market town. This is how Leicester grew to be an important Roman town with its own public baths—the remains of which can still be seen.

For the Britons who lived off the land, life was hard. Each year the pattern of work was the same. For a typical farming family in the south of Britain, it began in the spring. Ploughing the soil with a heavy, iron-shod wooden plough, removing stones and flints, applying animal manure to make the earth more fertile, before sowing with wheat, barley and beans.

As the weather grew warmer, the small, short-horned cattle were taken to upland pasture and sheep were gathered in to be sheared. A farmer in the south might have only a few cows and sheep, but in the north, where wheat and other crops were harder to grow, farmers kept large flocks of sheep and many cattle, not just for their milk and meat, but to provide wool, hide, sinew and horn.

Much of the summer was spent in making repairs to houses and fences, and clearing new ground to grow crops for the following year.

Harvest time was the busiest of all. Up at dawn and out into the fields with sickles to cut the corn. It was cut just below the ear when it was not quite ripe, gathered together and spread out to dry.

About a third of the wheat was kept for the next year's seed and stored in a granary raised off the ground to protect it from rodents and damp. (You can see the remains of a Roman, stone-built granary at Corbridge in Northumberland.) The remainder of the wheat was stored in wicker-lined pits in the ground.

In the autumn, sheep were turned loose on the stubble, and cattle were brought in and fed off straw and hay.

The ordinary farmer did everything for himself, with the help of his wife and children, his ponies or oxen which pulled the plough, and his dogs who helped to herd his cattle and guard his sheep. Everyday, the family had to collect wood for the fire, feed the geese and chickens, grind their corn with a stone quern, set traps to catch small animals and birds, collect honey from the hive, and prepare food. It was a busy life.

Many British families spun their own wool to weave into cloth, tanned hides to make leather, and even made their own clay pots. But for those with money to spend, or goods to exchange, all of these things and many more could be bought at local markets and fairs.

Although most of the people lived off the land, and many were very poor, Britain was not without its skilled craftsmen, wealthy traders and farmers, and powerful chiefs.

Well before the Romans came iron was smelted in the Forest of Dean, and lead and tin were mined in the west country. Craftsmen made beautiful ornaments in jet, enamel and bronze; and wheat, woollen cloth and hunting dogs were sold to foreign traders in exchange for fine German glass and French wines.

Blacksmith's tombstone   Yorkshire Museum, York
The Britons were skilled in the use of iron long before the Romans came. It was their most important metal and was used to make everything from saws, sickles, plough-shares and spears, to knives, hammers, axes and swords. It was so important that bars of iron were sometimes used in place of money and given in exchange for food and clothing.

The Roman army used it too, to make chains and tyres for their waggons, shoes for their horses, and hobnails for the soldiers' boots.

When this blacksmith died, he left enough money to have this carved tombstone erected over his grave. It shows him at work wearing a leather apron, with the tools of his trade, an anvil, hammer and tongs.

After the conquest of Britain by the Romans, people who lived in the far west and north continued to live off the land as they had done for centuries, but many of those living in the midlands and the south began to live in towns. Many of these new towns were built with the help of Roman army surveyors and engineers.

When the Roman army first came to Leicester they found a small, tribal settlement, defended with pallisades and ditches. It was the capital of the Coritani tribe. After building a fort there the Romans moved on, but the small settlement continued to grow. In time, a council chamber was built, a bath-house, large houses with mosaic floors and a large covered market with shops and stalls. One shop sold bronze pins and jewellery, another sold glass bowls and flasks which were made behind the shop. There was a tannery where leather was prepared and made into boots and shoes, and a pottery factory making tiles and cooking dishes. Most of these buildings have now gone, but you can still see the remains of the bath-house.

Lead water pipe Grosvenor Museum, Chester
A good supply of water was essential in Roman forts and towns. It was needed, not only for drinking, but to supply bath-houses and to flush public lavatories and sewers. (The remains of Roman sewers can still be seen at St. Albans, Lincoln, Bath and York.)

Sometimes, water was easily available from a spring or well, but if not, the Romans built aqueducts, dams and reservoirs and water was channelled or piped into the town. At Dorchester, water was brought from 18 kilometres away and at Lincoln, sealed pipes were used to bring water nearly two kilometres from a spring known as Roaring Meg.

Water pipes were made of stone, clay or hollowed-out wood, jointed with iron bands. This one is made of lead and bears the name of Agricola.

Lead ingot Grosvenor Museum, Chester
The Romans brought all lead mines under their control soon after their arrival in Britain. Lead was a valuable metal. The Romans extracted the silver from it, mixed it with tin to make pewter, exported it abroad and used it to make water-pipes, roofing materials, coffins and water tanks.

Slaves and prisoners-of-war were used to mine the ore, after which it was crushed, roasted, smelted and made into ingots or 'pigs' about 80 kilogrammes in weight: not too heavy to transport, but too heavy for a workman to steal. This lead pig came from the mines in north Wales. The letters—IMP.VESP.AVG.V.—tell us that it was made in the fifth Consulate of the Emperor Vespasianus Augustus, in A.D. 74.

The remains of another Roman town can be seen at Silchester in Hampshire. This was once the capital of the Atrebates, one of the British tribes in southern Britain. From the many objects that have been dug up there, we know that there was a tannery, an iron-smelting furnace, a pottery and a foundry, not to mention the workshops of dyers, coopers, leather-workers and carpenters. Many of the tools which the workmen used can be seen in the nearby museum at Reading.

The building of these new towns provided work for all kinds of people, not just stone-masons and carpenters, but shopkeepers, bath attendants and street-cleaners. Some people had slaves to work for them, and if the slaves worked well they could become rich enough to buy their freedom, or be given it by their master as a reward for loyal service. At the museum in South Shields, Tyne and Wear, you can see the tombstones of two slaves who were given their freedom. One, called Victor, came from north west Africa; the other, a woman called Regina from Hertfordshire, married her Syrian master.

Many of the things which the richer townspeople wanted had to be brought from other countries, to the ports of York and London. No large town would be without its foreign merchants who sold shiny Samian pottery from France, pickles, olive oil and anchovy sauce from Spain, and incense from Arabia.

In return, British and Roman traders exported corn and woollen cloth, wheat and hunting dogs. The Germans bought our enamelled brooches, and oysters were sent to Rome.

Within about 100 years, Britain was a thriving province, with bustling towns and busy ports. Many Britons accepted their new way of life, taking Roman names, copying Roman manners and dress, living in Roman-style houses, even sending their children to school to learn Latin—the Roman language.

Carpenter's plane   Reading Museum
This carpenter's plane was found at Silchester in Hampshire. The building of the Roman town there provided work for many people. Stonemasons, plumbers and labourers were needed to build streets, offices, temples, shops and houses. The materials used—stone, wood, lead, iron, clay for bricks and tiles, sand and lime for mortar—meant more work for quarrymen, foresters, miners and blacksmiths. Many of the skilled craftsmen who decorated the important buildings and large houses at Silchester with mosaic floors and painted walls, came from abroad, but they passed on their skills to the young British apprentices who worked with them.

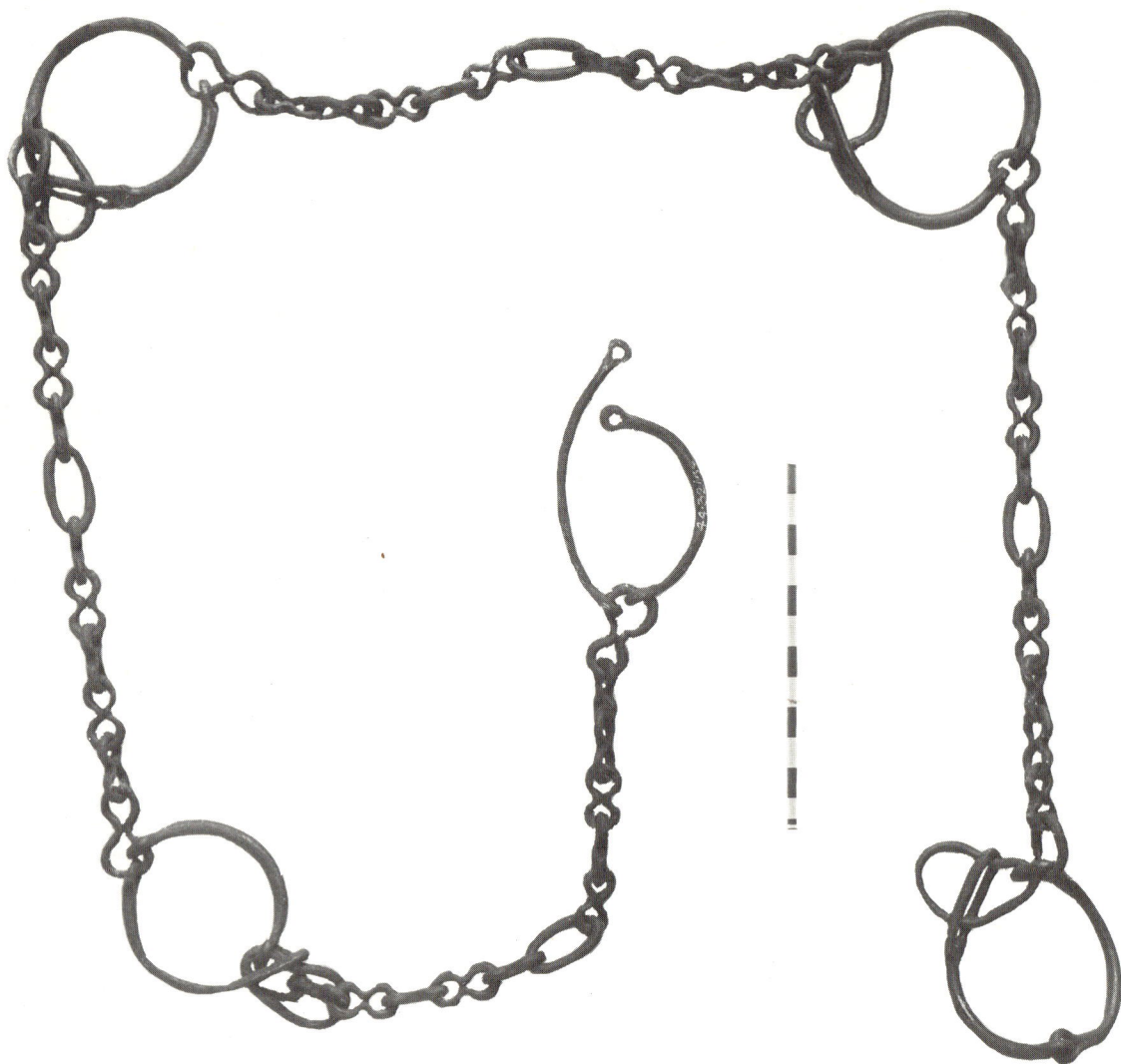

Slave chains   National Museum of Wales, Cardiff

Many people owned slaves in Roman Britain. These chains were once used to bind the slaves of a Welsh chieftain.

Some slaves were ordinary men, women and children who had been kidnapped and sold by slave dealers. Others were prisoners-of-war or criminals. Any children born to slaves became the property of the master and grew up in slavery. If too many slave children were born, some were left in the fields to die.

A slave had no rights. He could be bought and sold at a public auction like an animal. Many were badly treated by their masters and punished for the smallest thing. If a slave ran away and was caught the letters F U G (the first three letters of the Latin word for runaway—FUGITIVUS) were branded with a red-hot iron on his forehead. If the slave stole he was branded with the letters F U R, meaning thief.

4
At Play

Glass bowl   Ashmolean Museum, Oxford
This glass bowl from the famous glass-making town of
Cologne in Germany was found in Somerset. The
letters around the rim—VIVAS CUM TUIS PIE Z—
mean 'Long life to you and yours: drink and good
health to you'.

For many people who lived in Roman Britain there was little time for play. Servants in the towns, and farmers and their families in the country worked seven days a week, often from dawn to dusk, with hardly time to enjoy what simple food they had, let alone play games or listen to music.

Tragic Mask   National Museum of Wales, Cardiff
For the Romans, a visit to the theatre was a special treat. They liked to watch pantomines and listen to sad, Greek plays. But best of all, they loved the mime plays, where actors made fun of unpopular officials and politicians—as we still do today.

This small ivory carving shows the kind of mask which actors wore when they were performing a Greek play.

But now and again, even the hardest working people found time to relax.

Most Roman town dwellers, even those who could afford a bath-house in their own homes, would visit the public baths at least once a week, sometimes every day. The public bath was the centre of social life where people went, not only to wash themselves, but to hear the latest news and gossip. The baths which you can see at Bath in Avon are very grand, but smaller ones can be seen at Wroxeter in Shropshire. We know from the altars and tombstones which can still be seen at Bath, that people came from all over the Empire to take the waters—Priscus, a sculptor from Chartres in France, Peregrinus and Rusonia Aventina from Germany, a town councillor from nearby Gloucester, and Sulinus, a stonemason from Cirencester.

Townspeople with money to spend enjoyed visiting the theatre to see the latest pantomines and plays. Children liked to run around outside, visiting the stalls which sold sweets and cakes, and listening to the street sellers.

A very fine open-air theatre was built in St. Albans. There you can see the remains of the two great semi-circular walls which surrounded the theatre, and three large entrances which were once covered over.

The Great Bath   Bath, Avon
This large swimming bath, fed by a constant stream of water from the sacred spring, is just one of the baths in the public bath-house at Bath. Before going inside young men would stroll around the courtyard chatting with their friends and telling each other about their new girl friend. Some might wrestle or box, or play ball games. Old men would sit and discuss business matters and complain about the high taxes.

The different rooms in the public baths had different names. The undressing room was called the apodyterium. The cold bath was called the frigidarium. The tepidarium had a warm bath where servants and slaves massaged the bathers with oil. (The Romans had no soap.) The next room, the caldarium, was hot and steamy. Some bathed in the water, others sat and lay around on stone benches, whilst slave boys scraped the oils and dirt from their bodies with a scraper—called a strigil.

The audience sat on rows of wooden seats arranged in tiers around the central open space—called the orchestra. Important visitors, magistrates and priests sat in the orchestra itself, on a low crescent-shaped raised platform. (Even today, some of the best seats in a theatre are called 'orchestra stalls'.)

Plays and pantomines took place on the small, semi-circular stage. You can see it here between the remains of a standing

The Roman theatre at St. Albans
People who lived in or near St. Albans were lucky to be able to visit such a fine theatre as this. Even in a town without a theatre, people might sometimes be able to see a group of travelling players in the market square, a troupe of acrobats and jugglers or a man with a dancing bear.

column and a double wall. The column, one of five which stood over six metres high, marks the back of the stage (with changing rooms behind), and the gap between the double walls is where the front curtain was raised and lowered. The large, open space in front of the stage was sometimes used for religious festivals when children danced around a pole in the centre. The name 'orchestra' comes from the Greek word for dancer—'orchester'.

Some of the larger towns in Britain, especially those where soldiers were stationed, had an amphitheatre. (You can see a picture of the amphitheatre at Caerleon on page 59.) The word 'amphitheatre' means 'double theatre', so instead of being roughly semi-circular in shape, like the theatre at St. Albans, an amphitheatre is circular or oval shaped. At Caerleon, one might have seen fights between bears, wolves, dogs and wild boars;

A Chester

B Wroxeter

B Leicester

A Carmarthen

A Caerleon

A Cirencester

T St. Albans

B Bath

A Silchester

A Chichester

A Dorchester

This map shows where you can see the remains of theatres T, amphitheatres A, and public baths in towns B.

military parades; wrestling and boxing; or
fights between armed gladiators and slaves
or prisoners-of-war. A picture of a
gladitorial fight can be seen on a vase in
Colchester Museum.
(The map on page 47, shows where the
remains of public baths, theatres and
amphitheatres can still be seen.)

In the country, hunting and fishing were
favourite pastimes. Young British children
soon learned how to snare small animals,
how to kill birds with slings, sharp-pointed

Pottery vase   Colchester and Essex Museum
In the Roman amphitheatre, fights between armed
men—usually a gladiator against a prisoner—were
very popular. We know the names of the two fighters
shown on this vase because someone has scratched
their names around the rim. On the left is Secundus
Memnon, a Samnite gladiator from Italy. He is
heavily-armed with a rectangular shield, leg greaves
and helmet. His opponent, Salvenus Valentinus, seems
to have lost his net and dagger and his trident lies on
the ground, but he still wears a shoulder guard. He
holds up his finger, admitting defeat and begging for
mercy. If he has fought well, the president of the games
will give the thumbs up sign to Memnon and his life
will be spared. If not, the thumbs down sign will spell
his death.

darts, or a bow and arrow, and how to fish with rod and line. When they were older they hunted wolf, fox and deer. But best of all, the Britons—and the Romans too—enjoyed the danger and excitement of hunting the wild boar with mastiffs and hounds. You can see a picture of what a huntsman might have looked like, engraved on a glass bowl in the Ashmolean Museum at Oxford. He is seen dressed in a long-sleeved tunic and cloak, carrying a whip in his right hand. His two smooth-coated hounds are chasing a hare into a net.

Country people liked to sit around the fire and listen to a bard who played the lyre, sang songs, and told stories of heroes long ago. Others played a board game like chess or draughts. On long summer evenings children everywhere played among themselves, swimming and fighting,

playing football (or something like it), hide and seek, knuckle bones and noughts and crosses.

Townspeople and soldiers spent their evenings in a local cafe or inn, where they could drink cheap foreign wine and gamble with dice.

A wealthy Roman might invite his friends to his house for a special dinner party. Such a dinner would begin with oysters,

Toys from a child's grave   Colchester and Essex Museum
Young children in Roman days had many of the same kinds of toys which children have today—rag dolls, toy chariots (instead of toy cars), dolls houses, and rattles and enjoyed playing many of the same games—leapfrog, hide and seek, blind man's buff, and tiddly-winks. These small toys are from a Roman child's nursery. When the child died they were buried with her, to keep the child happy during her journey to the other world.

asparagus or snails fattened on milk. The main course, served on silver dishes, might be of pike livers, suckling pig or ham glazed with honey, which the guests ate with spoons and fingers. For pudding there would be ginger cakes, stuffed dried figs or pomegranates brought by sea from north Africa. Fine wine from Italy and France, sometimes mixed with water, would be served with each course. After such a grand meal, the guests were quite happy just to sit back on their couches and listen to a slave girl playing on the pipes, or watch a group of dancing girls—wearing the kind of bikini trunks like those you can see at the Museum of London.

Pottery mould   British Museum, London
People of all ages—especially boys and young men—liked to play ball games. We are not sure what kind of games they played. Sometimes it would have been fun just to play with a ball—as young children do, but both Romans and Britons might also have played games like football, hockey and handball. This naked figure on a pottery mould found in a Roman kiln at Kettering in Northamptonshire, carries what looks like a hockey stick.

The flute player   Reading Museum
Singers and musicians could always find work in a
Roman town. They were in demand for weddings and
funerals, for plays and pantomimes at the theatre and
for games and festivals. The most popular musical
instruments were the tuba (a kind of trumpet) and the
cithera (a small harp). Music played an important part
in religious festivals. Dancers kept time to the beat of
cymbals, tambourines and castanets. Horns and wind
instruments drowned the noise of animals as they were
sacrificed, and young girls, like this one, accompanied
the priests with the sound of pipes and bells. The
Roman army also had musicians. The most important
instruments were the bucina, shaped like a twisted
shell, the tuba and the cornu, a large circular
instrument made of bronze and horn.

5
At War

RVFVS·SITA·EQVES·CHO·VI
TRACVM·ANN·XL·STIP·XXII
HEREDES·EXS·TEST·F·CVRAVE
H · S · E

(Previous page)
Tombstone   City Museum, Gloucester
Soldiers from many different countries fought in the
Roman army—archers from Syria, stone-slingers from
the islands around the coast of Spain and horsemen
from France. They were called auxiliaries. In battle,
these lightly armed infantry and mounted archers or
spearmen were used in the front line to withstand the
first shock of the enemy attack. This tombstone once
marked the grave of an auxiliary cavalryman from
Greece. He was called Rufus Sita.

Maiden Hill, Dorset
This was one of the important hill forts used by the
Britons. You can read about a great battle which took
place here, and see a picture of one of the Britons who
was killed when a metal bolt pierced his spine, on page
16. If you look carefully at the picture below you will
be able to see the remains of a small, square Roman
temple in the top left-hand corner of the fort. This was
built in the late fourth century.

For a farming people, the Britons were
brave warriors. As a fighting force they had
many advantages over the Roman enemy.
In attack, their charioteers, lightly-armed
horsemen and foot soldiers could move
more quickly than the heavy-armoured
Roman legionaries. In retreat, they knew
the land well and could escape easily
through the thick woods and dangerous
marshes.

For centuries the Britons had defended
themselves by surrounding their farms and
settlements with ramparts and ditches.
Some settlements were quite small—just
large enough to contain a handful of
tribesmen and their families. Others, like
the great fort on Maiden Hill in Dorset,

with its three rings of deep ditches and steep ramparts, and two carefully planned entrances, gave protection to a whole tribe. (Other important defensive positions are shown on page 58.)

In the end, the Britons were no match for the disciplined Roman army of well-trained and hardened soldiers, many of whom had spent up to 20 years in the service of the Empire.

The main fighting force was made up of legionaries, all Roman citizens who had taken an oath of allegiance to serve the Emperor. The smallest unit was a tent party of eight men, who (as the name suggests) shared a tent. Ten tent parties made up a company or centuria, under the command of a centurian who led them into battle, together with the signifier or standard bearer. Six centuries made up a cohort and ten cohorts made up a legion, giving a fighting strength of about 5500 men. The first cohort was double the size of the others, and contained picked fighting men. Commanding the whole legion was a legatus or senator, assisted by six senior officers called tribunes and a camp prefect responsible for training and equipment. The senior officer below the rank of centurion was the standard bearer who carried the sacred symbol of the legion. The standard, surmounted with a gold or silver eagle, was closely guarded. It rallied the men in battle, and it was a disgrace if it was lost or captured. (At the Roman fort of Chesters on Hadrian's Wall, you can see the remains of the standard bearer's office, and beneath it is a strong room where the standard may have been kept in safety.)

In addition to the legionaries, each legion had up to 1000 foreign troops drawn from all parts of the Empire, called auxiliaries. They included spearmen, stone-slingers and mounted archers. Lastly, each legion had its own doctors and blacksmiths, clerks and carpenters, skilled armourers and engineers, not to mention musicians and priests.

Celtic shield   British Museum, London
The main weapons used by the Britons were the sword, the spear and the stone sling. (A well-aimed stone could kill a man at up to 90 metres.) Many tribesmen fought only with sickles and pitchforks. Their main defence was a small shield made of leather and bronze, although some warriors also wore helmets and body armour. This large, gilt-bronze shield, almost a metre in length and decorated with red glass, was found in the river Thames at London. Such a fine shield would have belonged to a chieftain. The main British attacking force was made up of light chariots drawn by two horses, with a driver and an armed warrior.

The uniform of a legionary   Grosvenor Museum, Chester

This is how a Roman legionary dressed for battle. Over a short-sleeved woollen tunic he wore body armour—overlapping metal plates held together by leather thongs and fastened with laces and buckles. His helmet, made of bronze and reinforced with iron, curves around his neck, ears and cheeks, to give added protection. His boots, thick-soled and heavily studded, are fastened with thongs around his ankles. Apart from his helmet and body armour his main protection is a rectangular shield, curved to fit the body. It was made of wood with metal strips bound around the edge.

Roman officer's sword   British Museum, London

This sword, with its finely decorated bronze scabbard, was once worn by a Roman officer. Apart from a small dagger, it was the only weapon which an officer carried.

The legionary soldier carried two main attacking weapons: a short, double-edged broad sword—called a gladius—used for fighting at close quarters, and a sharp, metal-pointed javelin—called a pilum—nearly three metres long. The javelin could kill at 30 metres, but more often than not it pierced the enemy's shield and stuck fast, making the enemy drop his shield and fight unprotected. Only if the legionary lost his sword would he draw his short dagger—called a pugio.

After 20 years service or more, soldiers received an official discharge diploma and a reward of money or land. Auxiliary soldiers were made Roman citizens. Some returned to their homes in Holland or Greece. Some married and settled in Britain and lived to tell their children of the battles of long ago. The tombstone of one of these auxiliaries can be seen at Gloucester. It shows a cavalryman in action, about to spear a Briton who lies on the ground. It was placed over the remains of Rufus Sita who served in the Sixth Cohort of Thracians for 22 years and died at the age of 40, far from his home in northern Greece. (The tombstones of other auxiliary soldiers who died in Britain can be seen at the Corinium Museum, Cirencester, and the Colchester and Essex Museum, Colchester.)

When the Romans were on the march in enemy country they built temporary camps. A temporary camp was just a square of land, large enough to contain the soldier's leather tents, surrounded with a ditch, a mound of earth and a fence of sharp stakes. The remains of such a camp, which may once have been used by the Ninth Legion, can be seen at Rey Cross in north Yorkshire. Sites of other similar camps are shown on page 58.

This map shows some of the military forts and defences which can be visited

For sites on Hadrian's Wall — see map on page 19
on the Antonine Wall — see map on page 21
For Saxon Shore Forts — see map on page 24

British hill forts and defensive positions
Castle an Dinas, St. Columb Major, Cornwall
South Cadbury, Somerset
Badbury Rings, Dorset
Hambledon Hill, Dorset
Hod Hill, Dorset
Maiden Hill, Dorset
Danebury, Hampshire
Caburn, Sussex
Warham Camp, Norfolk
Stanwick, North Yorkshire
Trapain Law, East Lothian

Roman marching camps
Y Pigwn, Powys
Rey Cross, Yorkshire
Chew Green, Northumberland

Roman Practice Camps
Gelligaer, Mid Glamorgan
Castell Collen, Powys
Toman-y-Mur, Gwynedd
Cawthorn, North Yorkshire
Burnswark, Dumfriesshire

Roman Legionary Fortresses
York, Yorkshire
Chester, Cheshire
Caerleon, Gwent

Roman Forts
Cardiff, South Wales
Caernarvon, Gwynedd
Brecon Gaer, Powys
Baginton, Coventry
Hardknott, Cumbria
Whitley Castle, Northumberland
High Rochester, Northumberland
Ardoch, Perthshire

Ardoch

Trapain Law

Chew Green
High Rochester

Burnswark

Whitley Castle

Rey Cross

Stanwick

Hardknott   Cawthorn

York

Chester

Caernarvon

Toman-y-Mur

Warham Camp

Baginton

Castell Collen

Y Pigwn

Brecon Gaer

Gelligaer

Caerleon

Cardiff

Danebury

South Cadbury

Hambledon Hill
Hod Hill

Caburn

Badbury Rings
Maiden Hill

Castle an Dinas

When the land was conquered more permanent forts were built. These were carefully laid out on level ground with deep ditches and high walls, strengthened with wood and turf. Later still, the forts would be rebuilt in stone. At Housesteads fort on Hadrian's Wall you can see the remains of the commandant's house, the headquarters building, barracks, a public latrine, a hospital and a guardroom. (Other fort remains are shown on page 58.)

The most important forts of all were the three great legionary fortresses of York, Chester and Caerleon. The one at Caerleon was the headquarters of the Second Augustan Legion. The first wooden fort was built there in A.D. 74–75, but it was rebuilt in stone over a century later. By that time, the fortress covered an area of 20 hectares (50 acres), with barracks, baths, offices, workshops, storerooms, stables and a hospital, carefully laid out in straight lines around the headquarters building and the temple in the centre of the fortress.

Roman amphitheatre, Caerleon
These are the remains of the amphitheatre, built in A.D. 80, which lay outside the south west gate of the Roman camp at Caerleon. It could hold up to 6,000 people and was an ideal place for holding military parades and ceremonials.

Even in peacetime the soldiers were ready to go into battle at any moment. They went on regular route marches in full armour and had daily training in sword fighting and spear throwing. At Tomen-y-Mur in north Wales, you can see the remains of a fort which the soldiers built for practice and at Burnswark in Dumfriesshire are the remains of earthworks used for a mock siege. (Other practice camp remains are shown on page 58.)

The Roman army fought many great battles in Britain and one of them took place in Scotland in A.D. 84. This was the battle of Mons Graupius.

Soon after dawn, the opposing sides took up their positions. The first line of the Roman army—8,000 auxiliary infantry, flanked by 3,000 cavalry—stretched out on the plain. Behind them, their backs to their camp, stood the main legionary force of 10,000 hardened soldiers, with more cavalry in reserve. Against them, on higher ground, stood the British—30,000 tribesmen—many barefoot and lightly armed with their main force of chariots in the centre.

Before the battle began, the two leaders made speeches to their troops. Agricola, the Roman commander, made fun of the enemy, calling them 'the Britons with the longest legs—the only reason they have survived so long', and ending by urging on the troops to crown their years of fighting 'with one day of splendour'.

The enemy chief, Calgacus, called on his men not to lose hope. 'Look at the Roman army,' he said, 'a strange mixture of nations that will surely be shattered by defeat. The gods have given them into our hands—like spellbound prisoners.' Then battle began.

After an exchange of stones, spears and arrows the Roman auxiliary infantry closed ranks and moved forward, pushing the enemy with their heavy shields and stabbing them with their swords. After routing the enemy chariots, the Roman cavalry also joined the fray. But the enemy stood their ground and those who had yet to join battle moved down the hillside to attack the Romans from the rear.

Agricola, quick to sense the danger, ordered his reserve cavalry to block their path. It was enough. The legions stood firm. The British retreated and were cut down by the cavalry as they fled. It was the end. As night fell, 10,000 Britons lay dead and wounded on the blood-soaked plain. The Romans, we are told lost only 367 men.

This was a battle in the open, but if the Roman army was attacking a well-defended hill fort or stockade, artillery was used. The Romans had two main artillery weapons. A light gun, called a carroballista, drawn by two horses, could fire arrows and iron bolts. Sometimes the arrows were wrapped in cloth, dipped in tar and set alight before firing. The catapult, called an onager, could hurl great boulders, 250 kilogrammes in weight, up to 400 metres or more. These catapults were often fixed on the towers of Roman forts, and at Burgh Castle in East Anglia you can still see the sockets on top of the towers, where the catapults were once mounted.

6
At Law

(Previous page) **The Roman road at Blackstone Edge near Rochdale**

The Romans built many straight roads between their towns and forts to make travelling easier and faster. Army engineers and surveyors decided how and where the roads were to be built, but all the heavy work was done by Roman soldiers and British tribespeople.

After clearing the ground of shrubs and trees, a ditch was dug on either side of the road to provide drainage and the soil from the ditch was put into the middle of the road to make a large mound—called an aggar. The aggar was first covered with large stones to make a firm foundation, then layers of small stones, flints or gravel were added.

This stretch of Roman road on the steep slopes of Blackstone Edge, near Rochdale in Lancashire, is paved with stones. The stone trough in the middle of the road is well-worn, probably by the brake poles of heavy carts as they came down the hill.

Other Roman roads are shown on page 65.

Under Roman law, the Governor of Britain was the Emperor himself, but since the Emperor could not stay in Britain all the time, he appointed someone else to act in his place.

The Governor was a very busy and important man. In addition to being the commanding officer of the Roman army in Britain, he was responsible for law and justice throughout the land and for keeping the Emperor informed of everything which went on in Britain.

To do all this, the Governor relied upon his legionary commanders, a permanent staff of officials, lawyers, secretaries and clerks and a personal staff of friends who he appointed for himself.

Anything to do with finance was the responsibility of another important official called the procurator Augusti, who was appointed by the Emperor. It was his job to collect all taxes, to pay the army and to make sure that the Imperial Estates (land, farms and mines owned by the Emperor) were properly managed.

The procurator made money in all kinds of ways. By renting shops in towns, collecting fines imposed by the courts, accepting bribes from people who hoped to get jobs with the government, selling land, digging for lead and copper, imposing custom duties on all goods entering and leaving Britain, and most important of all, collecting taxes.

There were two main taxes. A land tax based on how much a farmer or craftsman produced, and a poll tax based on how much land or money a person owned. On top of this, the Britons had to supply the army with corn and other goods which they needed.

Between them, the Governor and the procurator, with their staffs, were responsible for governing Britain. But they could not be everywhere at once. The Governor, as commanding officer of the army, spent much of his time on military matters. The procurator seldom left London—the financial capital of Britain. To make it easier for themselves, they encouraged the British to take care of their own affairs and they helped to build towns all over Britain to act as centres of local government.

The most important new towns were the four coloniae of Colchester, Lincoln, Gloucester and York, where colonies of Roman officials and retired soldiers settled down to live the life of civilized Roman citizens.

Each colonia was self-governing, and each had a town council of about 100 men. They, in turn, elected magistrates and officials to be responsible for law and order, for public buildings and water supplies, for keeping the streets in good repair, for collecting local taxes and assessing rates.

Other towns were built to serve the needs of the British. The Romans divided the country into tribal areas (rather like our present day counties), and each tribe had its civitas or tribal capital. (See page 14.)

The tribal capitals were governed in much the same way as the coloniae, by a council of important tribesmen who elected magistrates. Each capital was also allowed to send delegates to a national council (something like our parliament), where they could air their views and make complaints. The delegates had no power to make laws and the main purpose of the national council was to raise money for the annual festival in honour of the Emperor.

In some tribal areas, the tribal chief was made responsible for keeping law and order, collecting taxes and providing the Roman army with new recruits. One such chief was called Cogidubnus and the palace which he built for himself and his family at Fishbourne near Chichester can still be seen. It was one of the greatest palaces ever built in Britain, with courtyards and formal gardens, pools and fountains, painted halls and colonnades.

To make sure that laws were being obeyed, Roman legal officers paid regular visits to the towns and held courts where offenders were tried. For minor offences the punishment was usually a fine or a flogging. For more serious ones, ordinary people could be sent down the mines; important

(Overleaf) **Roman road near Hinkley in Leicestershire**

This is part of an important Roman road which stretched from Lincoln in the east, to Exeter in the south west. It is called the Fosse Way. Roads such as this made it possible for soldiers to move quickly from one fort to another in time of war. They made it easier for farmers and traders to carry their goods to and from markets and ports and they helped Roman officials to travel easily from town to town on government business.

Multangular Tower, York

Eburacum, or York, as we know it today, was one of the towns which the Romans built. It was begun in A.D. 71, as the army base of the Ninth Legion, but it soon became the military capital of Britain, an important centre of local government, a thriving port and a trading centre. When Britain was divided into two provinces, York became the capital of Lower Britain. Twice during the Roman occupation the Emperor himself and the Imperial Court were based here. Septimius Severus lived here from A.D. 208 to 211, and when Constantius I died here in A.D. 306, his son Constantine (later to be called 'the Great') was proclaimed Emperor.

Here you can see the inside of one of the fortress towers.

ROMAN ROADS IN BRITAIN

Some of the most complete remains are numbered.

1   Craik Cross Hill (between Moffat and Hawick) Scotland
2   Wheeldale Moor (south-west of Whitby) Yorkshire
3   Blackstone Edge, nr. Rochdale, Lancashire
4   Blackpool Bridge, nr Lydney, Gloucestershire
5   Fosse Way, north of Shepton Mallet, Somerset
6   Ackling Dyke, nr Badbury, Dorset
7   Holtye, Hartfield, East Sussex

people were sent into exile to some remote
province. For the most serious crimes of all,
the penalty was death by beheading,
burning or crucifixion. If a British offender
disagreed with his sentence, he could
appeal to the Governor. A Roman citizen
could appeal direct to the Emperor in
Rome.

One of the main duties of each tribal
capital was to pay for the building and
repair of roads. The thousands of
kilometres of roads were very important to
the Romans. (See map of Roman roads in
Britain, page 65.) They made it possible
for army officers and government officials to
travel quickly from one town to another,
passing on Government orders, collecting
taxes and keeping the Governor aware of
what was going on in the outlying districts.
In the towns and along the Roman roads
there were inns and relay stations where
official travellers could change horses or
find a night's lodging; and each town had
an official whose job it was to run the
Imperial postal service. The remains of once
busy inns can be seen at Silchester in
Hampshire and at Chesterholme in
Northumberland.

This system of government lasted for
almost the whole of the Roman occupation.
In about A.D. 200, Britain was divided into
two provinces; Upper Britain with London
as its capital and Lower Britain (so called
because it was the furthest away from
Rome) with a capital at York. Later still it
was divided into four provinces, and then
five.

But these changes hardly affected the
lives of most Britons who had grown to
accept the Roman way of life, and to
appreciate some of the benefits of Roman
rule.

7
At Prayer

In the life of the Britons, magic, religion and superstition played an important part. Each tribe worshipped its own gods. The god of sun and moon, earth and sky, a horned god of war who brought success in battle and the earth spirit who ensured good harvests and fertile cattle. The image of a fertility god, once worshipped by the Britons in Roman times can be seen in Dorset. It was carved into the chalk of a hillside near the village of Cerne Abbas. He stands 54 metres tall and carries a knotted club 36 metres long.

At certain times of the year great festivals were held. The festivals of Beltane at the beginning of May and Samain in November, are still remembered in our own May Day and Hallow-e'en. Led by their chief priests or Druids, the tribe made offerings to the gods to thank them for a good harvest, or to ask for protection through the long, dark winter. Sometimes a bull, a captured enemy or even a young child was sacrificed on a stone altar, and from the victim's spurting blood and twitching limbs, the Druids foretold the future.

Little is known of the Druids, but since they alone knew the ways of the gods, they were treated with respect by the tribespeople.

The Romans too worshipped many gods— Jupiter, god of rain, thunder and lightning, Juno, the wife of Jupiter and Minerva, goddess of wisdom—but the official state religion was the worship of the spirit of the Emperor. This was known as the Imperial Cult. Soon after their arrival in Britain, the Romans built a great temple at Colchester, in honour of Emperor Claudius, to serve as the centre of the Imperial Cult. (You can see the vaults of the temple on page 13.)

(Previous page) **Head of Medusa   Bath, Avon**
Many Romans came to visit Bath. Some came to bathe themselves in the healing waters, some to worship in the Roman temple of Minerva. High above them, as they entered the temple, they would have seen this carved stone head of a fierce gorgon.

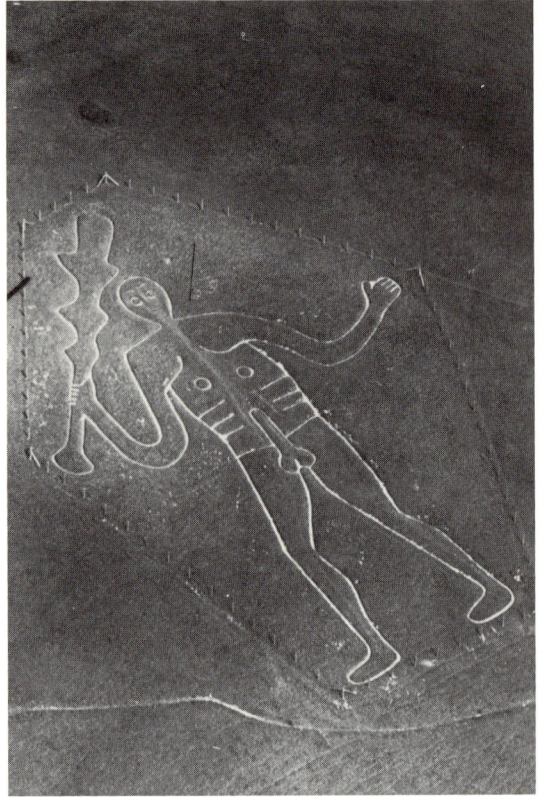

Chalk hill figure near Cerne Abbas in Dorset
Whoever carved this giant figure, or why, remains a mystery, but most likely the figure represents the god Hercules, and was carved by a local British tribe to ensure the fertility of their crops and cattle.

The Romans built many more smaller temples in towns and forts all over Britain. The best ones to visit are at Maiden Hill in Dorset, and Lydney in Gloucestershire; others are shown on page 70.

Even Roman houses had a small shrine or altar where the family worshipped its own household gods and spirits. The Lar was the guardian spirit of the house. The Penates watched over the larder and the storehouse. Vesta was the spirit of the fire; Janus, the spirit of the door; and there were special spirits who took care of children. At mealtimes, the head of the family placed wine on the altar and threw a piece of salt cake on the fire, as offerings to the spirits.

On special occasions such as a birth or a wedding, the household altar was decorated with flowers.

As a conquered people, the Britons were expected to show their loyalty to the Emperor, and to take part in Emperor worship. If they did this, they were allowed to go on worshipping their own native gods in their own way, for the Romans were a tolerant people who took care not to offend the native gods.

Many new gods were introduced by the soldiers and traders who arrived in Britain from distant parts of the Empire. At Carrawburgh on Hadrian's Wall, you can

see the remains of a small temple built in honour of Mithras, the pagan god of light, who fought against darkness and evil. Only men were allowed to worship there— usually soldiers and foreign merchants who were vowed to secrecy. There was a pit inside the temple, just large enough to contain a man. It was there that followers

Temple of Mithras at Carrawburgh
Of the three altars which you can see in the temple, the one on the left depicts Mithras, god of light. He is shown as a young man, naked except for a cloak, and carrying a whip, the emblem of the sun god. His halo is pierced with a hole through which torchlight shone, casting shadows in the darkened temple.

This map shows where you can see examples of temples, shrines and burial grounds

Remains of temples and shrines
2 Carrawburgh, Hadrian's Wall
4 Benwell, Newcastle-upon-Tyne
8 Caerwent, Gwent
9 Lydney, Gloucestershire
10 Bath, Avon
11 Cerne Abbas, Dorset
12 Maiden Castle, Dorset
13 Chanctonbury Ring, Sussex
14 Silchester, Hampshire
19 Colchester, Essex
21 London (Mithraic temple)
23 Lullingstone, Kent

Earth barrows
5 Hovingham, Yorkshire
6 Danes' Graves, Great Driffield, Humberside
7 Revesby, Lincolnshire
15 Thornborough, Buckinghamshire
17 Stevenage, Hertfordshire
18 Bartlow Hills, Bartlow, Essex
20 Mersea Island, Essex
25 Canterbury, Kent

Stone-built tombs and mausoleums
1 Chesterholme, Northumberland
3 High Rochester, Northumberland
16 Harpenden, Hertfordshire
22 Keston, Kent
24 Stone-by-Faversham, Kent

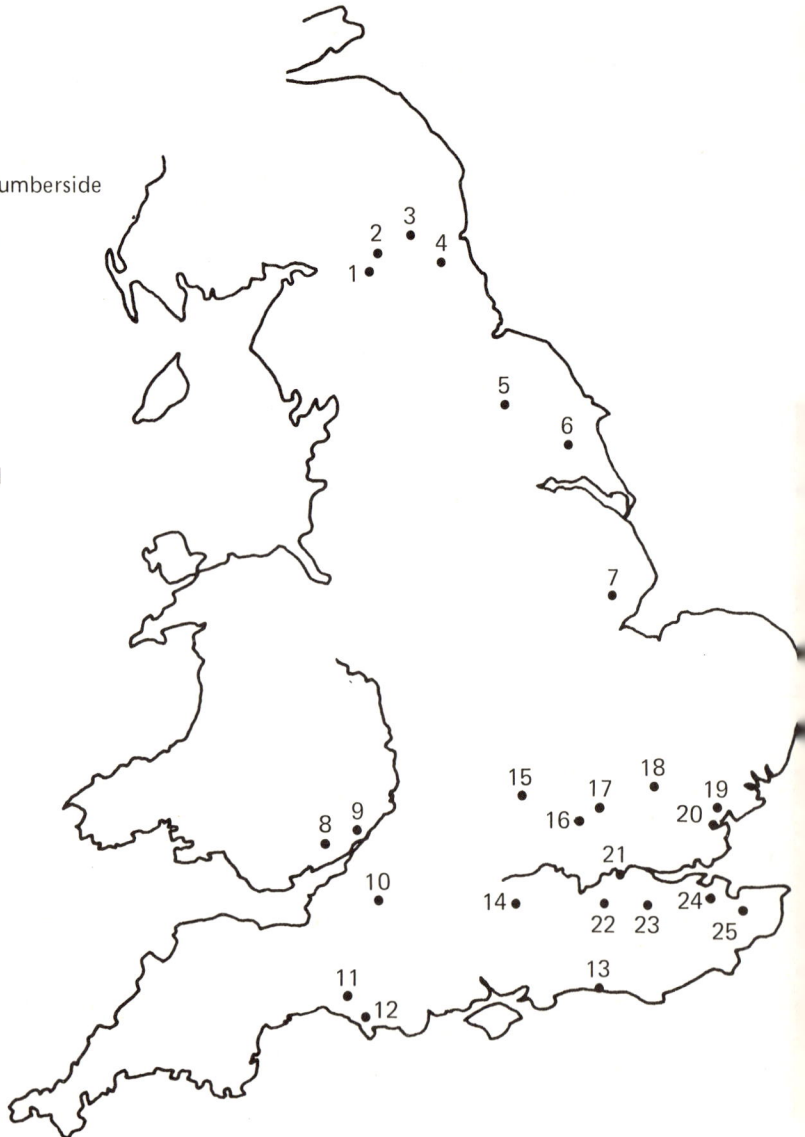

of Mithras underwent ordeals of darkness, heat and cold, to prove their courage and purity. Another Mithraic temple can be seen in London.

Other temples and shrines were built to honour the African god, Caelestis, and the Egyptian god, Serapis. (A dedication stone to Serapis can be seen at the Yorkshire Museum in York.) But in time, both Romans and Britains came to accept each others' gods and to worship them together with their own, as they did in the Roman town of Bath. Long before the coming of the Romans, Britons went there and paid homage to the spring goddess, Sul. For that reason, the Romans named the town— Aquae Sulis, the waters of Sul—and they dedicated their temple to Sulis Minerva, part British goddess Sul, and part Roman, Minerva.

Last of all, there came another religion from the East. It was called Christianity. We know very little about the first Christians in Britain, for they worshipped in secret. One secret chapel was found at Lullingstone, a villa in Kent (see the painting of the praying figures below); and the remains of a Christian church can be seen at Silchester in Hampshire. Other evidence of Christian worship comes from the use of the Christian chi-rho monogram ☧ , which is made up from the first two letters of the Greek word 'Christos'. We find it carved on a water basin at Chedworth and on a silver spoon in the Royal Museum, Canterbury.

Wall painting   British Museum, London

The early Christians in Roman Britain were often punished because they refused to take the oath of loyalty to the Emperor. They worshipped in secret and little is known about them. Early in the fourth century, the Emperor Constantine the Great gave them his protection and Christianity grew to become the most important religion in the Roman Empire.

One of the earliest Christian shrines in Britain was found in a villa at Lullingstone in Kent where one room was converted into a small chapel. These figures painted on the walls of the chapel, wearing beaded robes and with arms outstretched, show how the early Christians prayed.

Burial jar   Colchester and Essex Museum
Jars like these were often used to hold the ashes of a
dead person. It would be buried in the earth together
with food, money or personal possessions which
would remind the dead person of his life on earth, and
help him on his journey into the otherworld.

A child might be buried with its toys; a woman with
jewellery; a warrior with his helmet and sword.

The Romans took care to place money with the jar
which could be used as payment to Charon, the
ferryman, who carried the soul across the river Styx into
Hades.

Britons and Romans both believed in life
after death. The Druids taught that the soul
of a dead person left the body and lived on
in a new one. The Romans believed that the
soul passed on to live in the Underworld,
called Hades.

During the early part of the Roman
occupation, people who died were cremated.
Their body was burnt on a pyre and the
remaining ashes, after being washed in
wine, were placed in a container—anything
from a simple clay pot to a fine glass jar.
Sometimes the ashes were placed in a burial
jar with a face on it, like the one from the
Museum at Colchester.

Later, it became more common to bury
the dead in a coffin made of wood or stone.
The young girl's coffin from the Maidstone
Museum is made of lead.

Many graves were marked by nothing more than a wooden stake in the ground. Others, like the grave of Julia Velva from York, were marked with a carved tombstone. But only very wealthy families could afford to bury their dead in a stone-built mausoleum, or in an underground tomb covered with a high mound of earth. The burial mound at Mersea Island in Essex is said to be haunted by the ghost of the Roman centurian who is buried there. Other burial grounds are shown on the map, page 70.

(Overleaf) This tombstone from York was erected by Aurelius Mercurialis in memory of his wife, Julia Velva. It shows Julia lying on a couch, holding a cup of wine. In front, her daughter sits on a wicker chair near her small brother. A three-legged table between them is set with food for the funeral feast. Her husband stands on the right.
The first part of the inscription reads—
TO THE GODS OF THE UNDERWORLD AND IN MEMORY OF JULIA VELVA, A MOST DUTIFUL WOMAN. SHE LIVED FIFTY YEARS.

Lead coffin   Maidstone Museum
This lead coffin, found in Kent, was used to bury the body of a fair-haired young child. The parents must have been wealthy because the body was dressed in a silk gown and a purse, lined with linen, was placed by it. We know that the child was fair-haired because traces of fair hair were found inside the coffin.

D   M

IVLIE EVE PIENTISSI
ME VIXIT AN L AVREL
MERCVRIALIS HER FACI
VNDVM CVRAVIT VIVVS
SIBI ET SVIS FECIT

Some Museums of Special Interest

All of the pictures in this book show you things and places which can still be seen in museums, in towns, or in the country; and many other important places—towns, forts and defences, villas and houses, baths and theatres—are shown on maps 2–10. If you want to find out more about Roman Britain you might begin by visiting a local museum—here are some of the most important ones.

Aylesbury,
   Buckinghamshire Buckinghamshire County Museum, Church Street
Bath, Avon Roman Museum, Abbey Churchyard
Bedford, Bedfordshire Bedford Museum, The Embankment
Birmingham City Museum and Art Gallery, Chamberlain Square
Brighton, East Sussex Museum and Art Gallery, Church Street
   Bristol City Museum, Queens Road
Bury St. Edmunds, Suffolk Moyse's Hall Museum, Cornhill
Caerleon, Gwent Legionary Museum
Caernarvon, Gweynedd Roman Fort Museum
Cambridge Museum of Archaeology and Ethnology, Downing Street
Canterbury, Kent Royal Museum, High Street
Cardiff, South Glamorgan National Museum of Wales
Carlisle, Cumbria Tullie House Museum, Castle Street
Carmarthen, Dyfed Carmarthen County Museum

Chester Grosvenor Museum, Grosvenor Street
Chichester, West Sussex Chichester District Museum, Little London
Cirencester, Gloucestershire Corinium Museum, Park Street
Colchester, Essex Colchester and Essex Museum, The Castle
Corbridge, Northumberland Corbridge Roman Station
Coventry, West Midlands Herbert Art Gallery and Museum, Jordan Well
   Derby, Derbyshire Derby Museum, The Strand
Devizes, Wiltshire Devizes Museum, Long Street
Doncaster, South Yorkshire Doncaster Museum, Chequer Road
Dorchester, Dorset Dorset County Museum
Dover, Kent Dover Museum, Ladywell
Dumfries Dumfries Museum, Corberry Hill
Edinburgh National Museum of Antiquities, Queen Street
Exeter, Devon Rougemont House Museum Castle Street
Folkestone, Kent Museum and Art Gallery, Grace Hill
Glasgow City of Glasgow Museum, Kelvingrove; Hunterian Museum, The University
Gloucester City Museum, Brunswick Road
Hereford City Museum, Broad Street
Ipswich, Suffolk Ipswich Museum, High Street
Kingston upon Hull,
   Humberside Archaeology Museum, High Street
Lancaster Lancaster Museum, Market Square
Leeds, West Yorkshire City Museum

Leicester Jewry Wall Museum

Lincoln City and County Museum, Broadgate

London British Museum, Museum of London

Maidstone, Kent Museum and Art Gallery, St. Faith's Street

Malton, North Yorkshire Malton Museum, Market Place

Manchester City Art Gallery

Newcastle upon Tyne Museum of Antiquities, The Quadrangle

Newport, Isle of Wight Carisbrooke Castle Museum

Newport, Gwent Museum, John Frost Square

Norwich, Norfolk Castle Museum

Oxford Ashmolean Museum, Beaumont Street

Peterborough, Cambridgeshire Museum, Priestgate

Reading, Berkshire Museum, Blagrave Street

Ribchester, Lancashire Museum of Roman Antiquities

Rochester, Kent Public Museum, Eastgate House

St. Albans, Hertfordshire Verulamium Museum

Shrewsbury, Salop Rowley's House Museum, Barker Street

South Shields, Tyne and Wear Arbeia Roman Fort, Baring Street

Taunton, Somerset Somerset County Museum, Taunton Castle

Winchester, Hampshire City Museum, The Square

Worcester City Museum

York The Yorkshire Museum, Museum Gardens

More information about these and other museums can be found in a booklet entitled 'Museums and Art Galleries in Great Britain', published each year by ABC Publications, Dunstable.

If you want to find out more about places to visit, the following two books will be very useful—

R. J. A. Wilson Roman Remains in Britain *Constable* London

and

P. Clayton Archaeological Sites in Britain *Weidenfeld & Nicolson* London

and a very detailed map of Roman Britain is published by the Ordnance Survey, Southampton.

Remember too, that new Roman remains are being found almost every day. To find out more about these new finds, write to the Council for British Archaeology, 112 Kennington Road, London SE11 6RE.